GUNNISON COUNTY PUBLIC LIBRARIES

1 27 0000565703

CRESTED BUTTE LIBRARY
BOX 489
CRESTED BUTTE, CO 81224

D0933504

MUMMIES

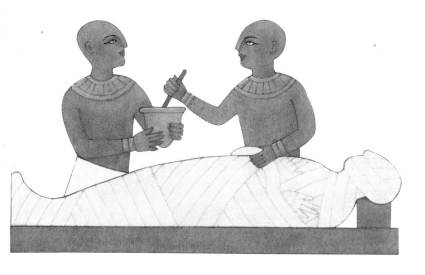

BY EDITH KUNHARDT
ILLUSTRATED BY KAT THACKER

To my wonderful daughter, Martha,
from her loving "Mummy"
E.K.

For Banshee (the pit kitten),
my favorite furry studio pal
K.T.

Special thanks to John McDonald, Egyptian Department,

the Metropolitan Museum of Art. Photo credits: facing p. 1,

CORBIS/Roger Wood; p. 39 top, Scala/Art Resource, NY;

p. 39 bottom, Egyptian Mummies by G. Elliot Smith and

Warren Dawson, courtesy of Kegan Paul International.

Library of Congress Cataloging-in-Publication Data
Kunhardt, Edith.
Mummies / by Edith Kunhardt; illustrated by Kat Thacker.
    p.   cm.— (Road to reading. Mile 4)
Summary: Describes how Ramses II, the powerful king of ancient
Egypt, was made into a mummy after his death.
ISBN 0-307-46402-4 (GB).— ISBN 0-307-26402-5 (pbk.)
1. Mummies—Egypt Juvenile literature. [1. Mummies. 2. Ramses II,
King of Egypt. 3. Egypt—Antiquities.] I. Thacker, Kat, ill. II. Title. III. Series.
DT62.M7K86 2000   99-35936
932—dc21   CIP

A GOLDEN BOOK · New York
Golden Books Publishing Company, Inc. New York, New York 10106

Text © 2000 Edith Kunhardt. Illustrations © 2000 Kat Thacker. All rights
reserved. No part of this book may be copied or reproduced without written
permission from the publisher. A GOLDEN BOOK®, GOLDEN BOOKS®,
G DESIGN®, and SHIELD DESIGN™ are trademarks of Golden Books
Publishing Company, Inc.

ISBN: 0-307-26402-5 (pbk)   A MM
ISBN: 0-307-46402-4 (GB)

CONTENTS

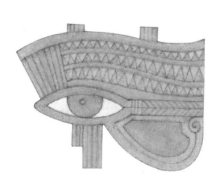

Econoclad 7.88 (101

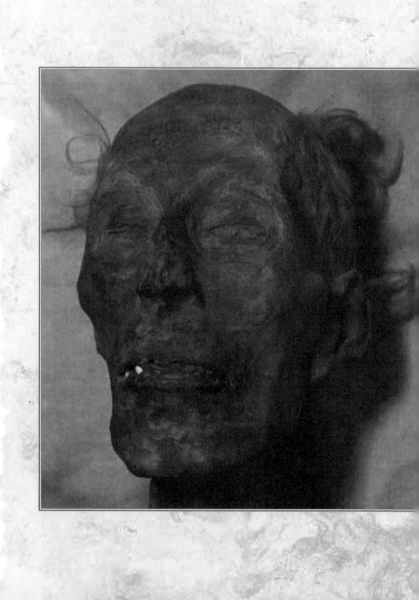

I

KING RAMSES

Meet Ramses.

Ramses died more than three thousand years ago. But there is still skin on his face and hands. There are teeth in his mouth. There is even hair on his head!

How is this possible? Most bodies turn into skeletons. Why didn't his?

Ramses's body was dried out and wrapped up. It was buried in a tomb. It lay hidden for thousands of years!

Ramses was made into a mummy.

Who was Ramses?

Ramses was a powerful king, or pharaoh (FEHR-oh), in ancient Egypt. He ruled Egypt for sixty-seven years. He is sometimes called the greatest pharaoh of all.

The people of Egypt mourned Ramses's death. But everyone was also happy for him. They knew he would live again.

Ancient Egyptians believed that

after people died, they started a new life in a wonderful place.

They called this place the Afterworld.

In the Afterworld, people could do all the same things they had done when they were alive. They could eat, drink, hunt, farm, and play. If they wanted, they could even go to war!

But they needed help finding the Afterworld.

Egyptians believed that when a person died, his spirit left his body. They thought the spirit looked like a bird with a person's head. After the body was buried, the spirit came back to guide the person to the Afterworld.

The spirit knew the person by his face and body—the way he looked when he was alive. A spirit would not recognize a skeleton. So if a person was going to get to the Afterworld, his body had to look the same after death. That's why the Egyptians made mummies.

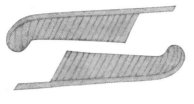

2

HOW TO MAKE A MUMMY

How was Ramses made into a mummy? It was not easy. And it took a long time—seventy days. First priests washed his body with wine. One priest wore a mask of a jackal, a wild dog. That was in honor of Anubis (Ah-NOO-biss), the Egyptian god of mummies. Anubis had the head of a jackal.

Ramses's brain was pulled through his nose with a hook and thrown away. His heart was left in his body. Egyptians believed that the heart, not the brain, did the thinking.

Now the priests made a cut in the side of Ramses's body. They took out Ramses's lungs, stomach, intestines, and liver. Each one was wrapped in cloth and put in its own special jar. The jars would be buried with the king.

Next the priests stuffed the body with packets of a special salt called natron (NAY-tron). They piled natron over the body, too. The natron dried

the body out so that it would last a long
time.

Work on the mummy stopped while
the body lay in the salt. But there were
other jobs to do. Craftsmen made jewelry,
furniture, games, and weapons.

The king would need all these things
in the Afterworld.

After forty days, priests took the body out of the natron. Now the skin was hard, like leather. It would not rot away anymore.

The priests rubbed the skin with perfumes and painted it with a sticky tree sap. Then they coated the body with red powder.

But the mummy was not done yet.

The priests stuffed Ramses's nose with pepper to keep its shape. They placed mud and sawdust in his body so it stayed round. Oils were rubbed into his skin to make it soft. All these things made Ramses look more lifelike.

Finally priests wrapped the body in cloth bandages to protect the skin. The arms and legs were wrapped one by one. So were the fingers and toes. It took fifteen days to wrap a mummy—and a lot of bandages. If you laid them out, the bandages from one mummy

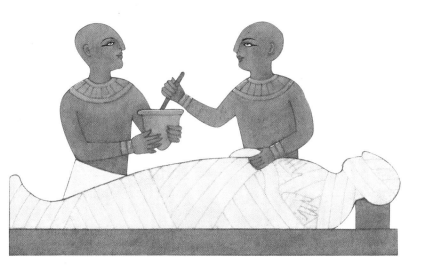

would cover an entire basketball court!

While they were wrapping the mummy, the priests kept stopping to say prayers and tuck amulets, or magic charms, into the bandages. The amulets would keep evil away, bring good luck, and protect the mummy on its trip to the Afterworld.

Sometimes there were as many as one hundred amulets tucked in the bandages.

The priests put sheaths of pure gold on the mummy's toes and fingers, right over the wrappings. A mask made of gold and rare stones was placed over

THIS BEETLE IS CALLED A SCARAB. LOTS OF SCARAB CHARMS ARE FOUND ON MUMMIES. EGYPTIANS CONNECTED THE BEETLE WITH THE RISING SUN AND NEW LIFE.

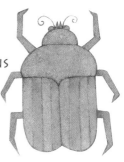

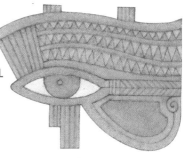

THIS AMULET GAVE THE MUMMY STRENGTH. IT LOOKS LIKE A GOD'S BACKBONE.

THIS EYE PROTECTED THE MUMMY. IT IS THE EYE OF A VERY POWERFUL GOD NAMED HORUS.

THIS AMULET IS ONE OF THE SONS OF HORUS. IT GUARDED THE MUMMY'S LIVER.

the mummy's head.

The face on the mask looked like Ramses's face. That way, if anything happened to the mummy, Ramses's spirit could look at the mask and still know who it was. The Egyptians weren't taking any chances!

The mummy was put in a coffin.

That coffin was put in a larger one.
Sometimes there were five coffins in
all, one inside the other. They were
covered with gold.

The mummy lay on its side with
its head on a headrest. An eye was
painted on the outside of the last coffin
so that the mummy could see out.

3

GOOD-BYE

Finally the seventy days needed to make the mummy were over. It was time to take Ramses's mummy to its tomb.

People came to say good-bye. Ramses's many wives pulled their hair. They threw sand over their heads. Tears ran down their cheeks. His sons and daughters cried, too.

Servants carried food, furniture, clothing—everything Ramses would need in his new life. Other servants carried statues of servants. Egyptians believed that these statues would come alive and serve the pharaoh in the Afterworld!

For centuries before Ramses lived, kings and some queens were buried in pyramids.

A pyramid was a huge tomb that was built to keep the king's mummy safe from robbers who wanted riches. The inside of a pyramid could be very

tricky. Sometimes there was a false hallway and trapdoor. Once the mummy was inside, the real way to the king's tomb was hidden and blocked over. But in spite of the tricks, no mummy was really safe.

There were about seventy Egyptian

pyramids in all. Every one of them was robbed and the treasures stolen. Some robbers were caught. Their punishment was death. But that did not keep others from trying. All those jewels and gold seemed worth the risk.

So many pyramids were robbed that

Egyptians stopped building them.
Instead they started digging secret
tombs in a valley in the mountains. We
call that place the "Valley of the Kings."
Ramses was buried in the Valley of
the Kings.

When Ramses's funeral parade

reached the entrance to the tomb, the priests stood the coffin up on one end. A priest performed the "Opening the Mouth" ceremony. He touched the face on the coffin with a special metal instrument. Now the mummy would be able to see, hear, talk, eat, and touch in its new life.

Inside the tomb, the coffin was carried down a hallway to a large room. Strong men lowered the coffin into a stone box and slid a heavy stone lid over the top. All the furniture, food, and gifts were left in the room. The hallway was blocked with stones. The door was sealed.

Now the mummy was alone. His new life began and would go on forever.

But for Ramses, "forever" didn't last very long. In about two hundred years, robbers broke into his tomb. They smashed open the stone box. They peeled the gold from the coffins. They tore off the golden mask and ripped the bandages apart to steal amulets. They took the four jars and dumped Ramses's organs on the ground.

When the robbers were done, the tomb was a mess. Ramses's mummy lay on the floor, all his riches gone.

Priests found the mummy and took it to the tomb of Ramses's father. They hoped it would be safer there.

Robbers broke into most of the secret

tombs in the Valley of the Kings. As far as we know, the tomb of King Tutankhamen (toot-ahnk-AH-men) was the only one that was not looted. It was hidden under another tomb and forgotten.

King Tut was not a very important ruler of Egypt. He was a pharaoh for only a few years. And he died when he was only eighteen years old. His name does not appear very often in Egyptian records. But today everyone knows it.

When Tut's tomb was opened in 1922, people were amazed. The gold was dazzling. The jewels shone like

stars. It was the greatest treasure ever found.

Imagine what treasure Ramses—the most famous pharaoh of all—had in his tomb!

And now it was all gone.

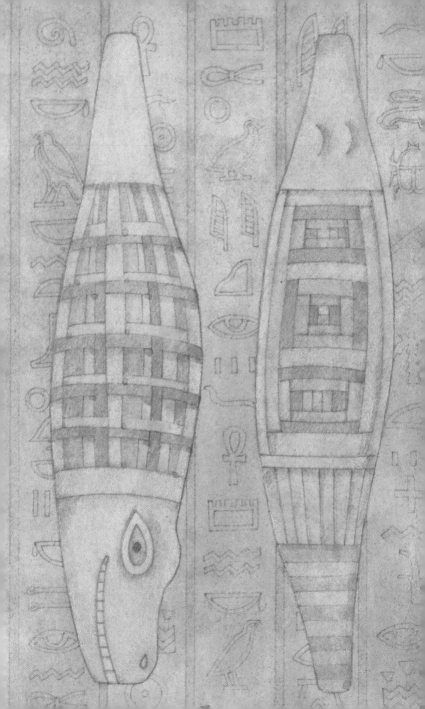

4

MUMMY POWDER

Egyptians made mummies for thousands of years. At first only pharaohs were made into mummies, then wealthy people, then anybody who could pay.

Millions and millions of mummies were made. Even animals were made into mummies!

Some Egyptian gods were connected to certain animals. That's why Egyptians made mummies out of these animals. Crocodiles belonged to Sobek, the god of water.

This bird-shaped coffin was for an ibis. An ibis mummy was a favorite offering to the god Thoth (THAWTH). So many millions of them were mummified that today the Egyptian ibis is extinct.

Sometimes people made their pets into mummies and put them in tombs. One tomb was found with a gazelle mummy inside. The gazelle was probably the pet of a little girl.

Egyptians loved cats. When a pet

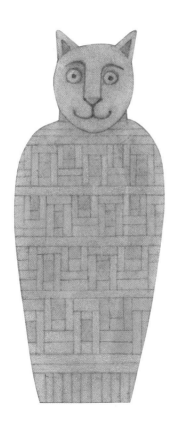

cat died, its owners often traveled to the city dedicated to the cat god Bastet. They put their pet's mummy in a cat-shaped coffin. Then they buried the coffin in a cemetery—for cats only!

What other animals were turned into mummies? Baboons, sheep, fish, ducks, and snakes. Even full-size bulls!

After thousands of years, the Egyptians stopped making mummies. Centuries later other people found the mummies. Here were bodies that seemed to last forever. Did mummies have magic powers?

Many people thought so. They ground up hundreds of thousands of mummies to make powder. They ate the mummy powder to cure stomachaches and fix broken bones. They rubbed mummy paste on cuts and bruises.

Some people even made fake

mummies. They put dead bodies in the sun to dry out and ground them into powder. Then they sold the powder as "real" mummy dust!

People found unusual new uses for mummies. They were burned like firewood, used to fertilize soil, and added to artists' paint to keep it from cracking. Mummies were even used as fuel for trains!

At one time, mummy bandages were made into paper for wrapping food. So many people got sick from eating the food that no more mummy paper was made.

In the 1800s, rich people even had mummy parties. The host bought a mummy and took it home. He invited all his friends over for the evening. Then, one by one, the bandages on the mummy were peeled away.

Sometimes a hand or an arm or a leg fell off when the mummy was unwrapped. Usually the people saved it. What a creepy thing to keep in a living room!

But where was the mummy of Ramses? When his tomb was found in the 1800s, the mummy was not there. It was missing. So were the mummies of other famous pharaohs.

Then, over a hundred years ago, three Egyptian brothers found about forty mummies in a cave near the Valley of the Kings. Long ago, after many tombs were broken into and robbed, priests had moved the mummies to this secret cave.

Ramses's mummy was found. So was the mummy of his father. Later the mummy of his son was found at another place. Do you think they look alike?

Ramses moved to a new home in a museum. But he still was not safe. The mummy had some green stuff growing on its neck.

Everyone worried about the ancient pharoah. The President of France offered to help. French scientists would try to "cure" the mummy.

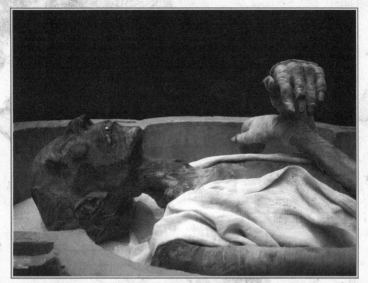

RAMSES

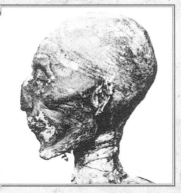

RAMSES'S SON

RAMSES'S FATHER

Ramses was given a passport. It listed his job as "king"! Then Ramses flew to France. The people there welcomed him like royalty, even though he had been dead for over three thousand years.

A team of twenty scientists tested the mummy. What was wrong? Soon they found out. A fungus was destroying the mummy. It was treated with radiation and cured.

Once the fungus was cured, the scientists had time to examine the mummy. X-rays were taken. They showed that many things had been wrong with Ramses. He had heart disease and arthritis in his hips. His back teeth were worn down. That was not unusual for a mummy. Many people had bad teeth because Egyptian bread was full of sand. But one of Ramses's teeth was so infected, it may have caused his death!

Today Ramses's mummy lies in a museum. Every day people come to see the great king and learn about his

life in ancient Egypt.

When they buried him, the Egyptian people wanted Ramses to live forever. And, in a way, he has. After three thousand years, his name has not been forgotten.

CRESTED BUTTE LIBRARY
BOX 489
CRESTED BUTTE, CO 81224